THE
INDUS
SOUTH ASIA'S HIGHWAY OF HISTORY

by JANE WERNER WATSON

Maps by Henri Fluchere

GARRARD PUBLISHING COMPANY
CHAMPAIGN, ILLINOIS

For reading the manuscript of this book and check-
ing the accuracy of its content, the author and pub-
lisher are grateful to Dr. Lyra R. Srinivasan, Social
Studies Coordinator, The Education Council, Jericho,
New York.

Contents

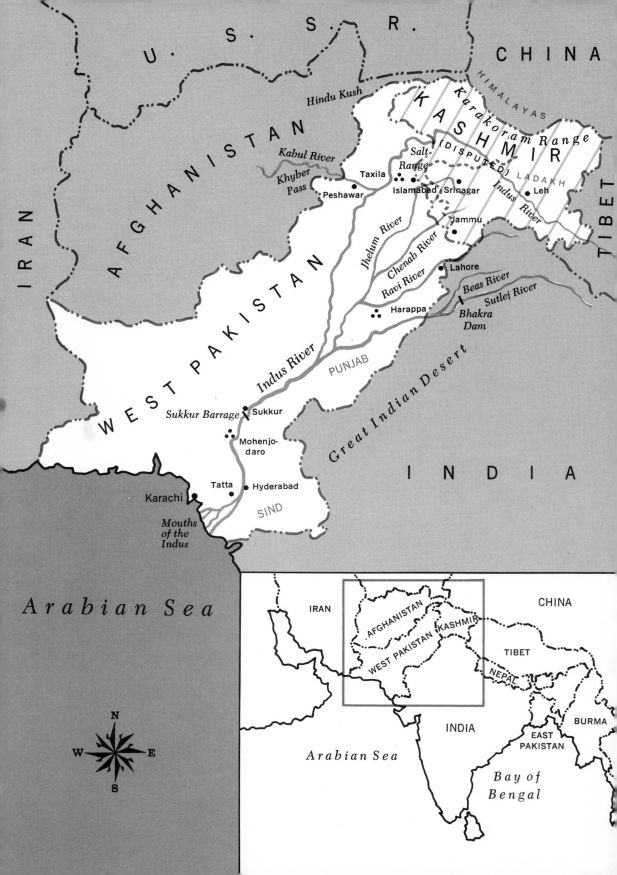

1. From the Snow Peaks

(Present Day)

The valley of the Indus River is shaped by mountains. They start from rough, bony slopes that almost tumble into the Arabian Sea. As one travels northward, the peaks to the west tower higher and higher until snowcapped tips of the Hindu Kush range glint against the sky.

Then, towering in a gigantic curve, a mass of white peaks sweeps from west to east. They back up the mighty Himalayas to form a high and icy barrier between West Pakistan and Kashmir on one side and China on the other.

Down the shoulders of these mountains, huge ice sheets inch slowly. During the summer months

Caravan men of the Himalayas pause for a rest.

meltwater drips from under the lips of these glaciers. Gathering into three small streams, this meltwater is the source of the Indus River.

For two hundred miles the young streams, first separately, then joining together, flow across high, bare, mountain-circled tableland of pale-tinted rock, gravel, and sand. A few stunted willows soak up moisture from the sandy banks, but this is dry countryside almost without trees, grass, or people. Between May and October a few showers may bring about three inches of rain. Winters are bleak and bitter, but there is not much snowfall on the windy tableland.

The high passes in the circling mountains are closed for the winter months by deep snows. But as soon as spring returns and warmer air melts enough snow to open the passes, the caravan men of the Tibetan trade routes begin to move across the tableland. Dressed in long robes, thick boots,

A caravan laden down with trade goods moves slowly through the mountainous country of Kashmir.

and fur-lined caps, these rough, cheerful cara-vaneers day after day plod beside their sturdy, long-furred, heavily laden yaks and small, tough, Tibetan ponies.

In this dry, empty country, caravans like to follow streams, for water is a treasure. Near the spot where the three small streams flow together to form the main stream of the Indus, two Tibetan trade routes join. A cluster of stone huts beside the river makes up the trading post of Tashigong, 15,000 feet above sea level, and one of the world's highest towns. At small posts like this, Tibetan caravans meet to exchange loads.

A few miles northwest of Tashigong lies the still-disputed border between Tibet, which is held by China, and India. Here army patrols keep watch over caravans as they wind along the trail beside the Indus. This country may seem desolate and unimportant to an outsider, but neither China nor India wants to give up a mile of it.

In 1954 the two countries signed a pact, prom-ising, among other things, to respect each other's territory. The problem is to decide to whom this mountain country belongs. China's maps show much of it as a part of China. India's maps, made by British surveyors when Britain ruled India, show the same territory as belonging to India.

Since the Communist Republic of China seized Tibet in 1950, it has built roads in a number of areas reaching toward India's borders. It has established military bases and airfields, and has sent bands of Chinese to settle on the high tableland of Tibet. These moves have made India uneasy.

In 1962 Chinese forces moved across the disputed territory at several points into land held by India. They seized Indian army posts, some in Ladakh near the upper reaches of the Indus. Since this boundary dispute has not yet been settled, the upper Indus has a new importance in international affairs.

To protect her borders, India has built a road through the main range of the Himalayas into the high country of Ladakh. The river has cut a channel through the mountains too. On the western slope of the Ladakh range, both road and river pass through Leh, the district capital.

Leh's stone-block houses have door frames painted red and blue. From some buildings sounds of school children chanting their lessons can be heard. It is only in recent years that going to school has become customary in the high mountains. Now Leh has both elementary and higher schools.

Poles carrying wires for electricity are beginning

This donkey and child are being brought across a mountain river on a rope bridge.

to appear in Leh too. A canal has been dug to lead river water through a small electric power station. The waters of the Indus are being used to bring some of the comforts of modern life to mountain folk.

In Leh a sturdy bridge of wood and stone crosses the Indus. This bridge seems wonderful to caravan men, for the bridges across many other mountain streams are just triple strands of rope. One strand is for the feet, another for each hand. Yaks and ponies often have to be fastened into slings and hauled across on other ropes suspended above the rushing water.

On the sturdy bridge in Leh the heavy whine of a truck is often heard. Truckloads of supplies for Indian army units come up this road during most of the months of the year. Outside the town on a gravelly flat, an airstrip has also been built. Airplanes sometimes appear between the peaks and skim down to difficult landings there.

Few of the people of Leh have ridden in a truck or jeep, though, and fewer still in an airplane. Men and women usually still walk wherever they go, carrying loads on their backs. They may sling a sack or two of grain over the back of a small cow, if they have one. More people keep sheep and goats, which eat rougher pasture and provide wool that can be traded for salt, sugar, and tea.

Wherever a slender thread of snow meltwater flows down a gentle slope, someone grows a tiny plot of barley. A small, twisted apple or apricot tree may loom above the barley stalks. A few beans or peas may be grown to add a little variety to meals of barley-flour cakes and tea made into a nourishing broth by the addition of butter made from yaks' milk. But the scant crops of this country cannot support many families. Ladakh district has only about two people per square mile in its 45,000 square miles of territory.

In this high country there are monasteries called lamaseries, which house the men who devote their lives to the worship of their gods, instead of marrying and having children. The men become lamas and learn to write and to read Buddhist holy books. They attend services lighted by the

The colorful inhabitants of Leh throng the main street of the little mountain town.

smoky glow of butter-oil lamps. To the throb of drums and the bong of bells they chant prayers.

Some lamas work in garden plots. Others learn to paint holy pictures or to fashion temple images. Still others learn to perform story-telling dances wearing painted masks, or they accompany the masked dancers with the clash of small cymbals, the bang of kettle drums, or the mournful toot of trumpets.

People of the high valleys travel long distances to see these religious dances. But they also have their own folk songs and dances with which to celebrate a family occasion or a good harvest. These celebrations are important, because mountain life is hard and simple. In spite of hardships, though, few people want to leave their homes along the high reaches of the Indus.

2. High Green Valleys

(Present Day)

Under the shoulder of a 25,000-foot peak called Rakaposhi in the high Karakoram Range, the Indus River turns southward. After flowing for 500 miles at an altitude of nearly 15,000 feet, the river drops 10,000 feet in swift leaps and tumbles.

Four or five thousand feet above sea level, in the mountains, there are many valleys ringed by the diamond sparkle of ice and snow. Each spring, small cold streams of water from melting snow fields begin to thread their way through pleasant meadows to join bubbling brooks. These mountain streams flow into one or another of the several great rivers that will join the Indus on its long journey to the sea.

One of these rivers, the Jhelum, flows down from the mountain valley called Kashmir. "An emerald set in pearls" is the Kashmiris' term for their land. The emerald is the green of the lake-filled valley where the Jhelum rises. The pearls are the white peaks above.

Rice grown by farmers in the valleys of Kashmir is a mainstay of the Kashmiri diet.

The waterways of Kashmir give the valley a special charm. Its lakes are shallow and weedy but beautiful when they reflect the mountain peaks. Even the water weeds are used by farmers of the valley. They pole small boats out onto a lake. Then they twirl the long pole to pick up a load of muddy weeds which they spread on a garden plot as fertilizer.

Some of these plots are known as floating gardens. They were started on rafts of reeds anchored to the bottom with posts and heaped with mud. Over the years a mesh of roots has attached most of them firmly to the lake bottom, but water still flows between the plots. Farmers tend their melons, tomatoes, and other vegetables from small boats.

Canals cover the valley in a network, connecting the several lakes and joining the Jhelum at a number of points. These canals are maintained and controlled by villagers who live beside them and whose fields the canals irrigate. A large rice crop provides a great deal of the food for the Kashmiris, and some grain and other crops are also grown on the irrigated fields.

The tall houses of Srinagar line the banks of the Jhelum River.

In the capital city of Srinagar, canals serve as some of the streets. For several miles the city's old wooden houses, often several stories high, crowd the banks of the Jhelum River and adjoining canals. Seven old bridges span the river, and others cross smaller canals. But the many bridges do not interfere with the busy traffic on the waterways.

The Jhelum is the only river in the Himalayas on which many boats are used, for it flows through a valley that is wide and level. Flat barges are loaded with golden grain to be moved downstream to market. Other boats loaded with fresh green vegetables and fruits move among houseboats moored close to the banks. Boatmen crouch on the pointed sterns of these long, slender craft, slicing the water with heart-shaped paddle blades. Even mail is delivered to houseboat homes by boats, painted bright red.

Traveling fruit and vegetable vendors on the Jhelum sell their produce from houseboat to houseboat.

Beyond the city, villages line the banks of the rivers, lakes, and canals. Their tall houses have walls of mud bricks set in timber frames. They are so large and handsome that it comes as a surprise to find that they contain little or no furniture.

Sheep and cattle occupy the ground floor of each house. The upper story is for the storage of grain. On the middle floor the family lives, sleeping on mats spread on straw, and sitting on the floor or on the packed earth of the dooryard.

Each household, like most Indus Valley homes, has a few storage jars for grain, a few cooking pots, water jars, and tea bowls. Every house in Kashmir has a mortar and pestle for husking rice. The mortar is a hollow stone bowl in which the rice is placed. The pestle is a long wooden pole that is thumped up and down on the grains until the husks are loosened.

Most Kashmiri women have a spinning wheel, and many men have looms on which they weave blankets and shawls of wool. Some men also do fine embroidery or knot carpets, especially during

Both Kashmiri men and women produce fine handcrafts. This man is designing a carpet.

the winters when there is little farmwork and fishing.

In winter, people in the high valleys such as Kashmir spend most of their time indoors, perhaps with a small bowl of glowing charcoal under their long robes for warmth. Their houses have no other heat.

Winter temperatures rarely go below freezing, for these Himalayan valleys are no farther from the equator than the most southerly states of the U.S.A. A temperature of 40 degrees can be quite uncomfortable though, if a building has no heat.

Homes in Kashmir and other mountain valleys have few comforts. Food is limited. Life is simple and often harsh.

Through the winter people dream of the spring when almond and fruit trees scattered over the hillsides burst into bloom. People of Kashmir like to boast of the delicious fruits of their valley— excellent wild plums and berries of many sorts. Apricots and cherries are also grown, and the small wild apples are sweet and tart.

In spring, too, the melting mountain snows flow down again to fill the wide rocky bed of the Jhelum. From the river, waters fill the canals that irrigate the valley fields. And the river itself flows strongly down from the mountains onto the high plain.

The Jhelum is only one of the five great rivers that flow down from the Himalayas to join the

Indus. The others are the Chenab, the 'Ravi, the Sutlej, and the Beas. Each of the rivers has its source on some high snow-covered mountain slope. Each flows through high valleys where people live their own proud, independent lives.

All these valleys are separated by high peaks. The passes through the mountains are clogged with snow for many months of the year, and travel is slow and difficult at any time. There has been little visiting among the valley peoples. Even today each valley has customs all its own. But they have one thing in common: through each valley a river flows down to the plain.

Meltwater from glaciers like this one feeds the Indus River.

3. Across the Plain to the Sea

(2500 B.C.–Present Day)

To reach the level lands below the foothills of the Himalayas, the Indus has had to smash a narrow gorge through a wall of rock. Once it has thundered through this gorge and passed the rounded dunes of the Salt Range, the river soon reaches a wide green plain called the Punjab. Here wheat grows well, cattle find plenty of good pasture, and excellent horses are raised. And it is here on the Punjab plain that the Indus is joined by its great tributaries.

Out of the hills they come with a rush. First the Chenab flows into the Jhelum; then the Ravi joins them. The Beas flows into the mighty Sutlej. Finally, they all join forces and flow together into the Indus. In their honor the high plain is often called the Land of the Five Rivers.

When the Indus reaches the Punjab plain, it is still 900 feet above sea level, but it is also still nearly 900 miles from the sea. A drop of one foot to the mile is not much, so the river slows its pace and spreads out over a wider bed.

As the Indus flows southward, the land around it becomes steadily drier. This is particularly true to the east, where a barren desert separates the river valley from most of India. Here the land would be worthless without the canals that spread water to wide fields. As still more canals are built, more of this desert can be turned into fertile farmland.

Near the Arabian Sea, the river fans out through many miles of swamp. It almost vanishes as a stream before it oozes muddily out to sea. These muddy mouths have been pushing gradually westward. During long centuries they have moved almost 200 miles. Where the main channel of the

These passengers are prepared for a long wait for their train.

Indus once flowed into the sea, the Gulf of Kutch now lies deserted, surrounded by miles of dreary salt marsh.

Until modern times, transport between the sea and the distant foothills was by fleets of river boats. For many centuries the Indus was the main highway up the valley, and it was lined with lively river towns. Today most goods and travelers go up and down the valley by railway instead of water.

Villagers going on a journey carry their food with them and also bedding in a bulky roll. By day they sit on wooden benches in crowded railway cars. At night they spread their bedding on the benches, on the floor, even on luggage racks—wherever they can find space.

Beyond the windows of the train, the life of the Indus Valley moves slowly past. Long straight canals stretch away toward the horizons, with paths running along their banks. On these paths small donkeys amble with riders seated on their rumps, feet almost touching the ground. A row of two-wheeled oxcarts loaded with grain or cotton waits behind a barricade at a crossing for the train to rattle past. Now and then a line of men holding bundles above their heads can be seen crossing a canal through waist-deep water.

In villages along the tracks, the houses are made of mud or mud bricks as they always have been, because building stone is very scarce. Men sitting in the sunshine outside their homes look up to watch the train chug by. Here and there a woman is seen, perhaps laying out chili peppers to dry in the sun. Or she may be holding a small child between her knees while she searches its scalp for insects.

Not far from some of these villages, low, flat-topped mounds rise up from the plain. These dusty, bleak mounds do not look exciting, but they hold the key to the long-ago past of the Indus Valley.

Archaeologists know that these mounds rising above flat land often cover the ruins of very old towns. As mud-walled houses melted in the rain or tumbled down from age, the people leveled off the ruins and built new homes on top of the rubble. Gradually mounds were heaped up.

Broken cooking pots and water jars, children's discarded toys, and worn-out furniture were often buried beneath the new floors. Sometimes a coin that had rolled into a crack was buried too.

At Harappa, near the Ravi River, in the late 1800's, workmen were hauling in material for the roadbed of a railway line, when a supervisor noticed that some of the fill seemed to be very old bricks of unusual shape. When he asked where the bricks came from, the workmen showed him a tumbled mound that rose some 60 feet above the plain. The supervisor knew enough about archaeology to recognize the mound as the probable site of a buried town. He reported the find, and archaeologists soon came to investigate.

Archaeologists like to start from the top of such a mound and dig down with care. The newest levels are, of course, near the top. Older ones are buried below. Layer by layer the broken bits and buried pieces can tell a great deal about long-ago life in the town.

Unfortunately, the mound from which the old bricks came to the railway could not be dug in an orderly way. For years villagers had been using it as a quarry for ready-made building materials. They had pulled out whatever bricks were easiest to reach, often from low down in the side of the mound. They had turned the levels topsy-turvy. The archaeologists found Harappa a rather disappointing site.

Then, in the year 1921, an Indian archaeologist was standing on top of another low mound, 400 miles down the Indus Valley from Harappa. He was poking about among the ruins of a Buddhist monastery. As he handled some of the loose bricks that had tumbled from the walls, he thought they looked somehow familiar.

He knew, of course, that the bricks were old. Few Buddhist buildings were constructed in India after 700 A.D. Still, these bricks looked even older than that—much older. The archaeologist thought they looked like the mysterious bricks of Harappa; and he was right.

Unlike the tumbled mound at Harappa, the

mound around the ruins of this old Buddhist monastery had never been touched by a pick or shovel. Villagers of the countryside called the place The Mound of the Dead, and they left it alone. This was a great boon to archaeologists. They went to work at the new mound, digging with care.

In the years that followed, other similar ruins were uncovered in the valley. Together they told the story of the great Indus River Valley Civilization that had been lost for more than 3,000 years.

Part of the mound of Mohenjo-daro (The Mound of the Dead) still stands in the background of these excavations.

The sturdy brick walls and paved streets of The Mound of the Dead, above, and figure excavated at another ancient city.

In the long-ago Stone Age, tribes of hunters are said to have lived in the hills that rim the Indus Valley on the west. Some of their stone hand-axes and remains of their shelters have been found there. As they learned to plant seeds and harvest crops, they moved down into the flat river valley. Here the land was rich, the soil had no rocks in it, and there was water nearby.

By 2500 B.C. some of their villages had grown into large Indus River Valley towns. Strong city walls of brick plastered with mud or limestone protected them against the flooding of the river.

In other lands, city walls were often built as protection against enemies. But no weapons of war have ever been found in Indus Valley ruins. Archaeologists believe, therefore, that the valley people lived at peace for many years in their brick-walled towns.

Workmen digging in the Mound of the Dead uncovered many tall brick house walls lining paved streets, with stone-lined sewers laid beneath the paving blocks. Some buildings had stairways inside, indicating that there had once been upper stories. Kitchens of homes had built-in wells and smooth work-counters. Bathrooms were much like those in prosperous valley homes today.

The largest buildings in town were tall, well-ventilated structures with ramps leading up to them. Traces of grain have been found in them, so archaeologists think that grain was the principal wealth of the people. Seeds found in their trash heaps tell us that they flavored their food with sesame seeds, and that they enjoyed the rich sweetness of dates and the juicy goodness of melons. They raised field peas as well as wheat and barley. And they harvested cotton fluff which they spun into thread and then wove into cloth.

Judging from the number of ornaments that have been found, the women of the town liked jewelry very much, as women of the valley still do. Rings, earrings, bracelets, and jeweled belts set with bright stones have been found in the ruins. Many of the stones in them are not to be seen in the nearby hills, so the cities of the Indus evidently carried on a lively trade with other lands along the Arabian Sea.

Pakistanis still travel on camel-back as did their ancestors in the excavated cities.

Each man of the valley apparently had a small stone seal with which to mark his possessions. Some seals had words carved into them, but no one today has learned to read the words. All the seals have small pictures carved into them, though, and these tell us a good deal about life in the valley.

There are pictures of people farming with humpbacked oxen. Camels, asses, horses, and water buffalo are shown carrying loads. Sometimes a man is pictured, dressed in a pointed bonnet and short robe, making an offering to a god. The gods and goddesses and sacred animals on the seals look very much like those Hindus still honor today.

Artists also pictured the wild animals that lived in the marshy jungles along the river—tigers, rhinoceroses, and elephants. The climate then was evidently much moister than it is today.

The cities of the Indus River Valley lasted for at least a thousand years. But about 1500 B.C., the ruins tell us, these great cities met a sudden, tragic end. Scorched bricks tell that homes were burned. It seems that almost everyone had fled before the cities were attacked and burned. But the bodies of a few families killed by violent blows have been found in the ruins. Apparently they were late in leaving and were caught by the invaders. There they lay in their abandoned city, buried by tumbling bricks and swirling dust, for 3,500 years.

4. Warriors from the Mountains

(1500–400 B.C.)

The warriors who fell upon the cities of the Indus 3,500 years ago, burning and killing, were strangers from the high country beyond the Sulaiman Mountains to the west. They were tall, sturdy nomads who had been traveling in family groups for uncounted years. Some walked across country, tending their flocks, while others rode in chariots, pulled by snorting horses. Like most nomads, they had little use for those who lived in towns.

When their wanderings brought them within sight of the Indus Valley, the old walled towns seemed to promise good hunting. Down into the valley the nomads swarmed with their flocks and their families, their flashing axes and horse-drawn chariots. They fell upon the weakened old cities and left them empty ruins.

These tribes, whom scholars call Aryans because of their language, were great fighters. But they also liked to sing and dance to the music of the flute, the lute, and the harp. Gradually they settled down in the valley, but they built no cities to replace those they had ruined. These newcomers to the Indus Valley preferred to live in villages made up of just a few families. There they enjoyed peace and order. They did not even bother to bar their doors, for it was not their custom to steal or to harm one another.

We know about their life because their stories, songs, and poems have been passed on for thousands of years and are still well known today. We know that the most honored people among them were their priests, who ranked even higher than warriors. Priests were the ones who memorized the many long and beautiful poems and songs, later called the *Vedas*, with which the Aryans worshiped their nature gods. The sun god was called Suraj, the god of fire Agni, and the god of war, storm clouds, and rain was known as Indra.

After many hundreds of years, the great cities of Mohenjo-daro (The Mound of the Dead) and Harappa and other cities of the Indus were lost to memory. But the god Indra was still called "The Fort Destroyer," apparently because he was supposed to have led his people to victory against those towering city walls of brick.

Khyber Pass, gateway to the Indus Valley and path of invaders

Through the centuries some of the Aryans moved on across the wide countryside of northern India. But in songs they still remembered the far-off mountains and the great Indus River Valley they had conquered long ago. Around the sacred fire their priests sang rousing hymns like this one in honor of their warlike god:

Let me sing then the brave deeds
*   of Indra, the Lord of the Thunderbolt.*
First did he slay the great dragon
*   that lay on the mountains.*
Piercing the rock with his
*   heavenly weapon from Tvastur,*
Smith of the gods, did he let
*   loose the waters.*
Then with a bellow like cattle the waters
*   rushed forth from the mountains*
To flow down the slopes
*   to the ocean so distant.*

The Aryans who remained in the Indus Valley had been living there for almost a thousand years, and the countryside had become prosperous again.

Camel caravans still cross the snow-covered Khyber Pass.

Then armies from Persia stormed down upon the valley. This was in the sixth century before Christ, when the Persian Empire under Darius the Great was at its strongest. From trading caravans the Emperor had heard of the wealth of the land of the Indus. He decided to conquer that rich land.

The Persian soldiers were hard-muscled warriors, armed with long, sharp spears and with bows and quivers filled with pointed arrows. The Aryans, after many years of peace, were no match for these curly-bearded hordes, and the valley of the Indus was soon added to the Persian Empire.

The land of the Indus was considered the richest

of all the provinces of Persia. Every year a caravan went over the mountains to Persia, carrying tribute to the Emperor—the equivalent of five million dollars in gold dust.

In spite of having to pay tribute, the land prospered under the Persian rule. It was the custom of the Emperors to choose local rulers to act as *satraps*, or governors. Many of the conquered Aryans also joined the Persian army, forming units of infantry, cavalry, and chariot troops. They kept the peace and supervised the building of good roads.

Soon trading caravans with their long rows of camels could travel more swiftly and safely than before. New towns grew up along the trade routes in the valley and in those mountain lands that separated it from Persia.

As the years passed, however, the power of the Persians weakened. Local rulers broke away and set up their own rule in the valley of the Indus. People of one river town fought the people of the next. No two rulers were willing to cooperate, even to defend their people against an outside foe.

5. Conquests Warlike and Peaceful

(327 B.C.–700 A.D.)

It was spring of the year 327 B.C. Across the high plain of the Indus Valley, news was carried that the great army of Alexander of Macedon was on the march.

"He rides at the head of his troop mounted on a prancing steed," travelers reported. "His skin is fair and his hair is like the golden mane of a lion. He has the spirit of a lion too. His army crushes all who stand against it."

Alexander had left his homeland in northern Greece six years before. He and his army had been storming across Asia, conquering everything in their path. They had crushed the Persian

Empire. Young Alexander dreamed of nothing less than conquering the world.

Now Alexander and his army made their way down through the Hindu Kush range toward the plain of the Indus. Where the Indus enters the narrow gorge that leads it to the plains, Alexander had his men build a bridge, and he led his troops across it. He was welcomed by the rulers of the first towns he reached. But when he marched confidently to the east, he found the Five Rivers of the Punjab, one after the other, blocking his path.

First he came to the Jhelum. On its far bank a young local ruler named Porus had drawn up his army behind a front line of 200 elephants. In the blackness of a rain-drenched night, Alexander and his men forded the river. They circled the elephants and attacked Porus from the rear.

After that victory, Alexander forced his weary men forward. But soon there was the Chenab for them to cross, and after that the Ravi. Each crossing was wet, muddy, tiring work. Between rivers there were long, rough marches. The men, worn out from years of marching and fighting, were tiring fast.

By the time they reached the Sutlej—running swiftly, deepened by rain waters and snowmelt—the Greeks had had enough. These hardy fighting men sat down on their weapons.

"We will go no farther!" they said.

A young man of the countryside came to talk with Alexander as he camped beside the river.

"Cross this one river," he said, "and all the wide, rich plain will be yours. Beyond this river rules an unpopular king, who will be easy to defeat."

But Alexander's men would not go on, so sadly he turned back. His dream of world conquest had been defeated, at least in part, by the many rivers of the Indus system. But he had planted a seed of glory in one heart.

The young man who had come to urge him on had been much impressed by Alexander. After Alexander's departure, he traveled about, visiting Greek army posts and the governors Alexander had appointed to rule the peoples he had conquered.

When word of Alexander's death in Babylon drifted eastward, the young man took it as a sign. Taking the proud name of Chandragupta Maurya, he started to build his own empire, on the pattern of Alexander's.

Chandragupta raised an army of his own. He took some cities on the northern plains, and soon defeated the weak king he had told Alexander about. From this start he went on to build the first truly Indian Empire.

These boats on the Indus River do not look very different from the boats of Chandragupta's day.

Within a few years Chandragupta ruled most of India as well as the Indus Valley. And he ruled it well. He let villagers handle their local governments, and he saw to it that everyone was cared for. His royal roads, with inns along the way for travelers, began at the Bay of Bengal in the east and climbed the gorge of the Kabul River in the west. He controlled the boats that sailed the Indus and the ships that went to sea.

Chandragupta had a grandson, Asoka, who was as great a ruler as he. Asoka conquered still more lands and added them to the empire. But it is not for the vastness of his empire that Asoka is remembered warmly today. After years of fighting he turned from warfare and vowed to kill no more. Instead, he turned to the work of spreading a peaceful religion, Buddhism.

The Buddha had taught that the way to have a contented heart was to live simply, to think good thoughts, and to do good deeds without any concern for rewards. This was the teaching Asoka now spread.

The old city of Taxila in the upper Indus Valley,

This figure of Buddha is worshiped in a Kashmir monastery.

where Asoka had ruled as a young man, now became a center for the teaching of Buddhism. Shrines and pillars and buildings erected by order of Asoka can still be seen in Taxila and at many other places in the upper valleys of the Indus system.

Word of the gentle, peaceful, unselfish teachings of the Buddha spread to caravan men who passed through this region. They carried the news up the river valleys, through the mountain passes, and across the high country to Tibet and China. Soon young men from these distant lands came to learn about Buddhism in schools of the Indus Valley—and elsewhere in India.

One of the great gifts of India to China, and through China to Japan, was the religion of Buddhism. And it traveled out of India up the Indus River's caravan trails.

6. Moslems, Mongols, and Moguls

(711–1857)

In the year 711 a fleet of small ships sailed up the Indus. They carried Moslem warriors, followers of the prophet Mohammed of Arabia. Mohammed taught that there was only one God, whose name was Allah. He told his followers to spread this word abroad, and to stop the worship of man-made images wherever they found it. This fleet sailing up the Indus was the advance guard of a great new conquering force.

Those first seamen conquered a few cities in the land called Sind, on the lower Indus, but did not stay to rule them. It was not until the year 1000 that more Moslems came to the Indus Valley. This time they were Afghans who swarmed down through the rocky Khyber Pass. During the next 30 years an Afghan ruler named Mahmud of Ghazni led his men on a dozen raids.

The people of the Indus Valley were Hindus. They worshiped many gods and goddesses. Some were the gods who had been worshiped in ancient Mohenjo-daro. Others were the gods of the Aryans. The Hindus made offerings to images of these gods and goddesses in their temples. This was against Moslem beliefs.

Moslem raiders felt they were doing a good deed when they burst into Hindu temples and flung to the ground images of goddesses and gods. In one rich temple, Mahmud of Ghazni himself is said to have pulled his sword from its jeweled sheath and struck the statue of a god a great blow. As it tumbled to the floor and smashed into pieces, jewels poured from it like colored water from a fountain. From each raid the Afghans carried home caravan loads of treasure.

Next to invade the valley was the Golden Horde of the Mongols, hard-riding nomad horsemen from far up in Central Asia. Their homes were felt tents, and they cared nothing for cities, or for men who lived quietly tending farms. Their work was warfare. And under their great leader, Genghis Khan, they had one of the best organized armies the world has ever seen.

Genghis Khan led his horsemen, armed with lances and with deadly bows and arrows, first down

Worshipers of the Moslem faith entering a temple. Moslems are in the vast majority in Pakistan today.

into China. Then he sent them across Asia to southern Russia. Wherever they went, they tumbled great cities into ruins and turned rich farming country into empty grazing land for their flocks and herds.

Then they headed for the Indus. It was summer, and the river was in flood when they reached it. An army of the Moslems, fleeing the Mongols, was trapped by the flooded river. With the mountains for shelter on one side and the river behind them, the Moslem forces turned to face the Mongol horde.

When they came upon the Moslems, Genghis Khan and his men were weary from hard riding and oppressed by the heat of the valley. These Mongols were men from cold northern uplands. They were used to wearing heavy armor topped with cloaks of fur. They were not prepared for the searing heat of summer on the Indus plain.

The Moslems fought desperately. For a time it seemed as if the Golden Horde was going down to defeat. But Genghis Khan ordered some of his weary soldiers to scale the cliffs and steep slopes

Tamerlane receiving a conquered Persian sultan

sheltering the Moslem army. A surprise attack from the mountains took the Moslems unawares and defeated them.

The Mongol leader sent a party across the raging Indus to scout for more cities to conquer. After a few days they returned, exhausted.

"The heat of this place slays men," they reported to Genghis Kahn.

Once again a conqueror of half the world turned back, defeated by the valley of the Indus. Genghis Khan and his horsemen rode up the caravan trails to distant Samarkand. His golden tents were seen in India no more.

In the late 1300's came Timur the Lame, a descendant of Genghis Khan, usually called Tamerlane. It was his ambition to outdo the conquests of the Golden Horde. He rampaged down from Central Asia into the Indus Valley, and rode across the plains of North India, burning and killing. Then back across the Indus and up the mountains he went. And he left behind him towers of skulls and whispered tales of the dark Prince of Destruction who had passed that way.

Sons and grandsons of Tamerlane became Moslems and settled down to living peacefully. But around their evening fires they still liked to listen to tales of those old-time conquests and the rich treasure trove.

One young prince who thrilled to these stories was Babur, a great-great-grandson of Tamerlane. When Babur grew up, he decided to follow the route of Genghis Khan and Tamerlane into the Indus Valley. But he planned to do more than rob and destroy; he planned to rule that whole vast land.

In 1525 young Babur, mounted on a steed with rich trappings, rode down the rocky Khyber Pass to found an empire. Babur and his people came to be called Moguls instead of Mongols. And their rule over the Indus Valley and much of India lasted until the last weak Mogul ruler gave up his throne in 1857.

During the rule of the Moguls, the emperors usually visited the Indus Valley only when they were on the move. Babur's son Humayun was a wanderer for most of fifteen years. He had been

Angels serenade Akbar the Great
in this old painting.

driven from his throne, and fled westward with his
wife and some loyal followers to try to find help
in Persia. So it happened that his son Akbar was
born in an a small fortress overlooking the Indus
River.

Akbar became the greatest of the six rulers
known as Great Moguls. He widened the empire,

but more important, he was as wise and good a ruler in peacetime as he was brave in battle.

Akbar and his men loved to travel. They moved from palace to palace across hundreds of miles, with long trains of elephants and horses. Where they camped, the canopies of their red and gold tents dotted the field like huge blossoms.

One of their favorite routes led up from the Punjab plains to the Vale of Kashmir, high on the Jhelum River. There they built palaces and

Pakistanis still enjoy the Shalimar Gardens in Lahore planned by the Mogul emperor, Shah Jahan.

laid out beautiful gardens in the Persian style, with streams and tinkling fountains among beds of bright flowers.

Another favorite palace of the Moguls was in Lahore on the banks of the Ravi River. It still stands in the walled fort above the city, many of its rooms opening upon gardens. In the walls of some rooms are set bits of mirror that reflect the flame of a single candle with a thousand twinkling lights.

The last of the Great Moguls, Aurangzeb, died in 1707. After that the hold of the Mogul emperors on their empire weakened. One after another, local princes set themselves up again as independent rulers, making it easier for the next great invader to conquer the whole land.

The next invasion started with the arrival of Portuguese explorers who made their way up the Indus. Sailors from Portugal had been visiting the southern coast of India since Vasco da Gama first sailed around the tip of Africa in 1498. But no Europeans had visited the Indus since the days of Alexander the Great.

The art of making fine rugs was practiced in the Sindi towns long before India became part of the British Empire.

In 1555, strange, high-prowed Portuguese ships explored the river as far as the busy trading city of Tatta. But they did not stay. It was traders of the British East India Company who came and remained in the Indus Valley. They established a trading post in Tatta, some years after the Portuguese had first explored the river.

Pottery and beautiful decorated tiles were made in the Sindi towns near Tatta. Carpets were knotted, and saddlebags were woven in handsome designs. Cotton cloth was woven and printed in bright patterns, and the women did beautiful embroidery. These goods were sold to foreign traders, and the people of the Sind were delighted to receive gold, silver, and coral in exchange. Their rulers also enjoyed oddities from Europe— printed books, paintings, clocks, glassware, and rich fabrics.

This desert area of the Sind was controlled by Moslem rulers known as *mirs* or *emirs* who made a profit from trade and also from farmlands.

The rulers gave farmlands to their friends and supporters. A wealthy landowner often held several villages and all the farms around them. The villagers had to dig canals to bring water to their dry fields. They broke up the hard soil with plows pulled by camels. Growing a crop was hard work; and when the harvest was in, most of it went to the landlords. In turn the landlords gave a share to the emirs, who thought themselves all-powerful.

But the British East India Company was expanding and wanted these prosperous lands. They sent their red-coated armies to crush the emirs.

And by 1843 all the desert country near the mouths of the Indus was controlled by the British traders.

Most of the soldiers in the East India Company's army were Indians. In 1857 they rose up against the Company and made a try for independence. Their children's children call this the First War for Independence; the British speak of it as the Mutiny of 1857. It was quickly suppressed, but the Parliament of Great Britain decided to take over this area from the British East India Company and rule it directly. Thus, after 1858, most of India, including the lower valley of the Indus and the Five Rivers of the Punjab, became part of the British Empire.

7. Outpost of Empire

(1858–1947)

British army units arrived by the shipload. Their forts appeared in the mountain passes at the head of the Indus Valley. Their camps sprang up on the outskirts of cities. Beside the camps rose streets of homes for the families of English officials, and around these homes English flower gardens were planted.

The Indus River Valley had seen many other invaders—Aryans and Persians, Greeks and Turks, Afghans and Mongols. But all the earlier new-comers had settled into the life of the country and made it their home.

The English were different. They had come out to do a job—to rule this land for the benefit of the British Empire. But they still thought of England as home. They sent their children to school in England, and they looked forward to returning there themselves.

These men—the Viceroy who ruled in place of the Queen of England, the governors and district commissioners—were really working for England, but they told themselves that modernization would help India too.

A governor general turned the first sod for a railway up the Indus Valley, which did speed up transport. It largely replaced the fleets of slow river boats that had carried goods for thousands of years up and down the valley's main highway, the Indus River.

Other railways were built. They carried raw materials to seaports to be shipped to English factories, and they carried manufactured goods from England out to local markets for sale. This caused a great change in the life of the valley.

The cities along the river—Tatta, Hyderabad,

Lahore's Main Bazaar is still an important trade center.

Multan, Lahore and others—had long been busy manufacturing centers. Pottery, cloth, tiles, metal tools, and many other kinds of goods had been turned out by skilled craftsmen in small workshops. These goods had gone to market in the slow riverboats, on creaking oxcarts, or piled on camelback. They had been sold in countless small towns of the Indus Valley. The makers, the transporters, and the shopkeepers all profited from this trade.

These farmers are preparing cotton for the ginning machine.

Now cotton from the fields along the Indus was shipped to mills in England. Silk from Kashmir and wool from mountain sheep went to England to be woven or knitted. Many Indian looms stood empty. Workshops closed. Many craftsmen of Indus towns—and elsewhere in Greater India— had no jobs. Families drifted back to farms, where they thought they would at least have food.

When the British took over the government of India, they found almost half the people living and working in towns and cities. Before the

British left, less than a hundred years later, one out of every three town families had drifted back to the farming villages. More than 75 percent of the people depended on agriculture for a living, and that living was growing poorer.

Family plots around the villages became smaller and smaller as more people had to share the fields. Millions of people had neither jobs nor land.

Large landowners owned dozens of small plots and collected part of each farmer's crop as rent. In many cases these payments were so large and the crops were so small that families went hopelessly into debt.

As the years passed, most of the people of the Indus Valley and their neighbors throughout India became poorer and poorer. Their cities began to decay, and among the ruins lived hordes of people without hope.

The English realized the need to improve the country. They built dams and canal systems to make better use of the waters of the Indus River system. Before their work was done, more than 40,000 miles of canals lay like a great blue net over the countryside. Now water was at hand for much of the almost rainless land that had not been farmed before. People by the thousands moved in to plow new fields.

Tending the network of canals and the low dams called barrages, took many trained workers. The English sent out teachers and set up schools to train young Indian men to work on the canal system, the railways, and in government offices. Indians also joined the army under British officers.

There were still some wealthy Indian families in the country. Many of them sent their sons to England for higher education. These young men saw how the cities of England were growing and prospering as factories hummed. When they came home, it saddened and angered them to see how poor their country was.

These young men felt that the crafts and industries of their people were being destroyed so that Britain could prosper. They felt that the new dams and canals helped farmers to raise more crops just to support the British forces in the land. They felt that their people were losing their proud old culture as well as their independence. So the young men began to organize for freedom.

In 1895 the Congress Party was founded in India. Party members wrote newspaper articles against English rule. They held public protest meetings and urged people not to buy English-made goods, to encourage Indian manufacturing again.

The English jailed some of the freedom fighters and sent others out of the country into exile, forbidding their return. They also gave more government posts and responsibilities to local people in an effort to keep the peace. But they could not stop the movement toward freedom.

After World War I an English-educated lawyer named Mohandas K. Gandhi came home to India and became the leader of the independence movement. He ate and dressed as simply as the poorest peasant. To teach the value of the old ways, he learned to spin cotton on a hand spinning wheel, and he made his followers learn too. He won the love of the people by his fearless yet non-violent leadership.

Mr. Gandhi came to be called Mahatma, or "Great Soul," by his countrymen. He wanted to lead them all together—Moslems, Hindus, Christians, and others. Many thousands of all faiths did follow him. They marched the roads with him and joined in non-violent protests, even when it meant going to jail. But so deep a split had developed between Moslems and Hindus that not even the love and leadership of Gandhi could bridge it.

For several hundred years Moslems had been rulers over most of India. Even after the Mogul Empire declined, Moslems ruled many states in which most of the inhabitants were Hindus. The British permitted at least 500 of these princes to stay on their thrones, Moslems and Hindus alike. But it was mainly Hindus who were willing to attend the English-run schools and who manned government offices under the British. There were also many more Hindus than Moslems in Greater India—though not in the Indus Valley.

Though the proud Moslems were as eager for freedom from Great Britain as the Hindus were,

The great Badshahi Mosque in Lahore, built by Mogul Emperor Aurangzeb, is a symbol of Moslem dominance in Pakistan.

they feared a free India in which Hindus would have control. In 1906 they formed an organization of their own, called the Moslem League, to work for independence and Moslem rights.

One of the League's early leaders was Allama Iqbal, who had grown up in the town of Sialkot, in the foothills near the Chenab River. That was

Moslem country. In fact in the nearby Northwest Frontier Province 95 percent of the people were Moslems whose freedom, religion, and manner of living were very dear to them. They could not bear to think of being ruled by Hindus. Iqbal grew up sharing these feelings. He was a thoughtful young man who liked to write poetry, but he also had studied law in England.

In 1930 Allama Iqbal was president of the Moslem League. It was then that he first spoke in public about his dream of a separate free State for the Moslems. "I would like to see the Punjab, the Northwest Frontier Province, the Sind, and Baluchistan made into a single State," he said.

This dream gave a new goal to the Moslem League's struggle for independence.

An earlier leader of the League, Muhammed Ali Jinnah, had felt that Hindus and Moslems must work together for liberty. Under the British, many small states that had often quarreled among themselves had been united under one government and one set of laws. Jinnah felt it would be a mistake to give up this unity.

Jinnah had been educated in Moslem schools in Karachi, near the mouths of the Indus, before going to England to study law. When he became interested in politics, he joined both the Moslem League and the Congress Party in which he worked with Hindus. As an early president of the League, he had tried to have it work with the Congress Party toward common goals. But as years went by and freedom came closer, rivalry and hard feeling between followers of the Moslem and Hindu religions deepened. Mr. Jinnah was won over to the proud dream of a separate Moslem nation to be called Pakistan.

Jinnah, first Governor General of the Dominion of Pakistan, as he watches the prime minister sign his oath of office.

Moslem leaders—even Allama Iqbal before his death—could see that dividing the country would cause many difficulties. Even so, the Moslems became more and more determined. Speaking once more as president of the League, Mr. Jinnah said, "No power on earth can prevent Pakistan from coming into existence."

By the end of World War II, the British realized that they could not hold onto Greater India any longer. But when they agreed to leave India in 1947, they did try to persuade the leaders to keep the country unified after it became independent. Mahatma Gandhi and Jawaharlal Nehru, Congress Party leaders, were desperately anxious to avoid the partitioning of India. They offered to make Mr. Jinnah the first leader of a unified India, but Jinnah felt that he could not turn back.

So one hot August midnight in 1947 the flags of the British Empire in India were lowered for the last time. The flag of free India and the flag of the new Moslem nation of Pakistan went up to replace them.

8. Free but Troubled Waters

(1947–Present)

It is always difficult to draw boundaries to divide a country. The partition of Greater India was especially difficult because the two main units to be separated were the Moslem and non-Moslem populations. For hundreds of years they had been intermingled. They had lived side by side on almost every street of every town. Where could boundary lines go? Any lines would be certain to leave millions of families and their homes on the wrong side. Hindu families would find themselves in the new Moslem nation of Pakistan, while families that wanted to be part of the new Moslem state would be on the other side of the border.

Before independence, the British had met with Hindu and Moslem leaders to decide on the division of the lands directly controlled by the British. In East Bengal, a thousand miles east of the Indus, Moslems were in the majority. This state became East Pakistan. Most of the lower Indus Valley became West Pakistan, separated from the eastern part of the new nation by a wide stretch of India. In the Punjab hills, where the Five Rivers rose, there were more Hindus

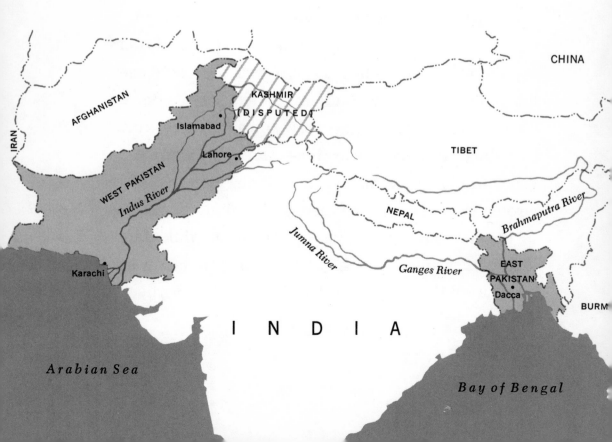

than Moslems. Much of the hill country, therefore, went to India.

More than 500 states, large and small, were still more or less under the control of their old rulers, called maharajahs, nawabs, or nizams. Each of these rulers was given the privilege of deciding whether his state should go to India or to Pakistan.

Rulers generally decided on the basis of the religion followed by the majority of their people. If most of the people of a state were Hindus, the ruler felt that he must join India even though he himself was a Moslem. But there were exceptions.

One exception was the mountain state of Kashmir, far up the Indus. Though 85–90 percent of the people there were Moslems, the ruler was a Hindu. He could not make up his mind to join Pakistan, though his people might have chosen it.

In another very large independent state far to the south, the opposite was true. The ruler of the state of Hyderabad, one of the wealthiest in all India, was a Moslem. More than half his people were Hindus. The Nizam of Hyderabad did not want to join either India or Pakistan. He felt that his prosperous state could do very well as an independent country. But the Indian army marched quietly in, took possession, and firmly, though without violence, pushed Hyderabad into the Indian nation.

Rather naturally then, many people felt that Kashmir should go to Pakistan. Its people were loyal Moslems. Its rivers provided much of the water for West Pakistan's "life blood," the Indus River. The main road from the plains up to the mountain valleys of Kashmir ran through Pakistan. Still its ruler, the maharajah, hesitated.

Men of the nearby mountain states in Pakistan became angry and impatient. Finally, having decided to take things into their own hands, they shouldered their rifles and moved over the border to take Kashmir for Pakistan by force.

Then the maharajah called upon the Indian army for help. Hastily he signed a paper which said that Kashmir would join India. The Indian army moved in, taking much of Kashmir. Only a small part in the west continued to be held by Pakistan.

The struggle over Kashmir was so bitter that the matter was submitted to the United Nations for settlement. The United Nations decided that when the state was peaceful again all the people should be allowed to vote, to choose between India and Pakistan.

Somehow the time never seemed right for this vote. Because feeling continued to run so high it seemed likely that planning for the people to vote would cause violence to break out again.

After some years the state legislature of the joint state of Jammu and Kashmir voted to join India. And India considered the matter settled.

Pakistan did not. It felt that the people of Kashmir had a right to vote on the matter, and that they would choose Pakistan. Several times in recent years this feeling has caused the flare-up of active fighting.

In many states ruled by princes, there was no problem about deciding which new nation should be joined. But even in areas over which there

Moslem families crowd aboard this locomotive of a train bound for Pakistan from New Delhi.

was no dispute, there was a terrible time when masses of people had to leave their beloved homes—Hindu families heading for India, Moslem families for Pakistan.

Millions of people were uprooted and unhappy. In this troubled time all the bad feelings that had lurked in hearts for many years boiled to the surface, resulting in burning, looting, and cruelty.

Crowds rioted in the streets of the cities. Smoke rose over towns and villages as shops and homes by the thousands were burned. Trains moving toward the border, filled with fleeing, homeless families, were stopped by armed bands and help-less passengers were murdered.

The leaders of both nations tried to calm their people. But the riots were out of hand. Prime Minister Jinnah of Pakistan fell ill and in 1948 he died. As he said his twilight prayers in the garden of a friend, Mahatma Gandhi of India was murdered by a bitter young Hindu.

More people died during these difficult times than have died in most of the world's great wars. And even today, to guard their borders against each other, India and Pakistan spend great sums of money on armies they can ill afford.

When an uneasy peace settled down, Pakistan did not even have a capital. It had the lovely green city of Lahore on the Ravi River, with wide avenues shaded by tall trees and fine old palaces. But Lahore was too close to the troubled border to serve as a capital. The seaport of Karachi was used for some years, but it was very crowded and also hot.

The Pakistanis decided to build a new city called Islamabad, up in the foothills of the Himalayas, where the weather was cooler. A stream flowing into the Indus was dammed to form a lake, and a new community of homes, schools, and government buildings was laid out among the fields, woods, and orchards of fruit trees. The new city represented the spirit of the future for the Land of the Indus.

A crowded street in Karachi

The modern buildings of Islamabad loom behind these two men and their burro.

9. Salt on the Fields

(Present Day)

"What we got in partition," men of Pakistan say with a smile, "was a desert and a swamp."

The "swamp" was the fertile, damp, rice-growing delta of the Ganges and Brahmaputra rivers. This delta makes up the Pakistani state of East Bengal. The "desert" was the almost rainless valley of the Indus, a thousand miles to the west.

The farmers of the Indus Valley were dependent on river waters, spread through irrigation canals. But Pakistan realized that even its river waters were not safe. The Indus and all the five great rivers of the Punjab either rise in India or flow through Indian territory on their way to the plains. If India dammed those rivers, it could starve the people of West Pakistan.

With help from the United Nations the needed Indus Waters Treaty was worked out and signed in 1960. About 10 million people in India depend on these waters, and about 40 million in Pakistan. So it was decided that about 20 percent of the waters could be dammed up for use in India, and 80 percent should flow down to Pakistan.

The upper waters of the Five Rivers are being well used. On the Sutlej River in India stands Bhakra Dam, 740 feet high, one of the dozen tallest dams in the world. It provides power for making electricity and fertilizer, and through many hundreds of miles of canals irrigates hundreds of thousands of farm acres. Another dam for power and irrigation spans the Beas River, high in India's hills.

Across the Jhelum River in Pakistan stretches Mangla Dam, an earthfill dam more than a mile wide. The Tarbela Dam across the upper Indus will be wider still. Both will produce electric power and irrigate vast farmlands.

Bhakra Dam on the Sutlej River will help to irrigate 3,600,000 acres of land and provide electric power for the valley.

On the west side of the Indus Valley, a dam across the Kabul River was completed some years ago by Pakistan. And there have been low barrages and canals down the valley, irrigating millions of acres, for many years.

Much of this irrigation system was developed by the British, beginning more than a hundred years ago. But over the years something strange happened beneath the surface of those rich fields.

The canals were unlined, so a great deal of water seeped slowly from them down into the soil. An engineer says, "It was like covering the country with a leaky sieve. The water drained away through the sieve of canals, leaving behind salts."

The salts coated the surface of the ground with glistening white grains. Most plants will not grow in salty soil, so more and more farmland became useless for crops. By 1960, 100,000 acres each year were being lost to cultivation, ruined by salt. This was tragic for farm families.

As water drained away through the walls of 40,000 miles of canals, the underground water

A farming expert examines the parched soil and tries to find a way of improving crops.

table rose. In the year 1900 this underground layer where water is stored was nearly 100 feet below the surface. That was fine. But the water table rose at the rate of about a foot and a half a year. By the 1940's and 1950's the water was coming close enough to the surface so that the soil in many fields became soggy and waterlogged.

The irrigation system on which farmers of Pakistan had so long depended was turning on them like a great soil-destroying monster! The government of Pakistan asked for help, and teams

New methods and better irrigation have produced a bumper crop on this Punjab farm.

of engineers from several countries, including the United States, went to study the problem.

They decided tube wells would be the best treatment. Crews were soon at work digging. The soil was deep, fine sand with no rock to slow the teams. "Well digging was as simple as cutting butter," an engineer says in describing the work.

Down went the wells. In went pumps. Soon the pumps were pouring streams of water back into the canals. Down went the water table, so fields were not waterlogged any more. Pumping doubled

Farmers of the Punjab bargain with dealers for the best price in grain markets like this one at Karnal.

the supply of water in the canals, so there was twice as much water to be used for crops—and to wash down surface salts. Many farmers began to grow two crops a year on fields where they could grow only one before. Crop yields were soon up 150 percent.

Government-dug tube wells have been improving a million acres a year. Farm extension workers have gone up and down the valley, encouraging landowners to dig their own tube wells. Groups of farmers have joined in cooperatives to dig more wells. In recent years these privately dug wells have almost matched those dug with government help.

The villages of the Indus Valley look much as they have looked for hundreds of years. Slim towers of mosques still pierce the blue sky. And in the south a few date palms nod their feathery heads above the pale mud walls.

The people have not changed much. They still like to sit outside their houses in the sunshine. Men talk about their crops and perhaps puff on a water pipe. Now and then they look up when a

Farmers use these bullock carts to take their crops to market.

pair of carts comes racing down a dusty track, the drivers standing up to whip their horses and shout encouragement.

At harvest time these carts bring in sacks of grain that pile up beside village streets. Sugar cane stalks taller than a man are cut and ground up for their sweet juice. Mounds of fluffy white cotton picked by women and girls tower as high as village house walls. Fruits from nearby trees are heaped in baskets in the markets.

At night a pale gold moon still looks down on the glitter of water in a thousand canals. From the distance sounds the *chunk-chunk* of pumps. And on the tree-shaded tracks along the banks, bullock carts creak by. With their hand-carved planks and wooden wheels, the carts have not changed in design since days of Mohenjo-daro. While their drivers nod in sleep, the placid bullocks plod patiently through the night. They are carrying to market crops that are the sign of a brighter day dawning in the long, long story of the valley of the Indus.

Index

Picture credits:

Meet the Author

JANE WERNER WATSON brings to writing about the Indus River not only the background of her scores of books for children, but a warm personal acquaintanceship with the land of the Indus and its tributaries. With her husband, a student of the scientific development of the area, she has visited West Pakistan several times during the past decade and has lived for several years in India.

The Watsons' interest in ancient history and archaeology has led them to the ruins of 4,500-year-old cities along the Indus, and to 2,000-year-old Taxila on the high plain. Their interest in modern science has taken them to dams, barrages, canals and salt-encrusted fields to study irrigation methods.

They have visited the Indus and the Five Rivers of the Punjab at many points from the Arabian Sea through desert, plain, and foothills to mountain valleys. They have driven up the Khyber Pass and Kabul Gorge, and up the high road to Ladakh as far as was permitted. And everywhere they have met and enjoyed the people of the Indus.